Flirt with Life

The Only Way Out

Tapan
Ghosh

Republished in 2022 by
BecomeShakespeare.com

One Point Six Technologies Pvt Ltd.
119-123, 1st Floor, Building J2, B - Wing, Wadala Truck Terminal,
Wadala East, Mumbai, Maharashtra, India, 400022.
T:+91 8080226699

Cover designed by Tushar More

Visit my website at www.tapanghosh.com

ISBN: 978-93-5610-121-0

This book is dedicated to everyone in my life who taught me not to take life seriously.

CONTENTS

What is flirting with life?

It is beyond comprehension.

You can only experience it by living life to the fullest.

Don't take life seriously; learn to flirt with it.

ABOUT THE BOOK

The title of this book comes from the way I have lived my life - by flirting with it. Attachment bogs you down and limits you as an individual. I live life to the fullest, always looking to do things I have not done before. All my learning comes from doing, not merely reading.

This philosophy has helped me grow beyond the confines of education, profession and society, and explore my creative side. I seek expression in writing stories and making short films.

'*Flirt with Life*' is my third book, after '*Faceless – The Only Way Out*' and '*An Anglo-Indian in Love*'. As with my previous books, there is a bit of me in here too, but in the form of quotes, thoughts, observations and beliefs from a lifetime of flirting with being an engineer, entrepreneur, patent holder, son, husband, father, creator and love guru!

DESTINY

How you are born is your destiny. How you die depends on how you leverage its course.

Our intent is in our stars. Destiny is always favourable provided your efforts are in the right direction.

If the wind was always favourable, the sailor would have no role to play.

The sailor in you must be in harmony with his fate to leverage the winds and navigate skilfully.

What is life but a journey across a vast ocean! And like any journey, it is full of highs and lows.

Calm waters and at times outrageous seas, or the rising swells and crystal-clear horizon. These conditions are extraneous features of the journey. They are a part of it and you, as the traveller, have little control over them.

The difference lies in the approach. The truth is that you have no control over them at all. They are the pre-drawn lines on your palm. You are born with one and it is an inalienable part of your life. It exerts its influence over you all the time. The difference lies in our approach. Like one sailor who blames the weather all the time or another who makes the best use of the weather conditions.

Therein lies the difference. Some of us complain all the time, like the poor sailor who believes he can do no wrong, it is never his fault. Likewise, some of us never accept the fact that we have been wrong, or could have done things better. *We easily end up blaming others for our pitiful condition, our failures and our shortcomings.*

Planning the voyage and preparation of the course is the key. A good sailor knows that he can encounter all kinds of weather conditions when he sets sail. He prepares himself before embarking on a journey and uses favourable conditions to make quick progress. He knows that there may be times when he has to slow down due to rough weather and sudden storms.

Our progress in life depends on our attitude. Like the wise sailor, if we refrain from cribbing and chiding, we can make our journey more meaningful.

Have faith in fate. Your destiny is tailor-made for you.

Destiny is a fait accompli, have faith in fate.

To surrender is to have faith in your destiny.
Don't try to fight destiny. Go with the flow.

Have faith in fate. You don't have a choice.

Have faith in fate. It delivers. Neither early, nor late.

Don't we say everything happens for the best? Then one must rely on this perspective.

Faith in fate is nothing but faith in yourself.

Whatever happens to you is destined. How you react to it is the question.

Not having faith in your fate is akin to not trusting God.

Having faith is important. In what is immaterial.

Having faith is important. In what and who is different for different souls. Let us accept this fact.

Faith is rooted in your inner self, else it's not faith.

When you say you are losing it, it actually means that you are losing faith in yourself.

Things always happen for our good but most of the time, we fail to recognize the boon in disguise.

Patience comes only with confidence, the origin of which is conviction in oneself.

Nothing you own is yours to enjoy unless you are destined to savour it.

Why spend energy to fight destiny when you can use it to go with the flow?

Surrendering means having faith in fate. Enjoying what you do without being anxious about the outcome.

Why grudge destiny when it is tailor made for each individual?

Do we understand the premise chosen for us?

Only when you have faith in fate will you respect others for their faith.

GETTING THE BEST OUT OF AN ASTROLOGER

Astrology is a divine subject, much misunderstood because we fail to apply logic to it.

An astrologer should follow up by finding out the result of his prediction to ensure greater accuracy the next time.

Don't expect the astrologer to know everything. He is not the messenger of God.

The accuracy of an astrologer's prediction lies in you telling him everything about yourself honestly. It's like consulting your doctor or a lawyer.

To get the best out of an astrologer, we must first know everything about ourselves.

Some of us tend to take the astrological readings for granted, while others think of astrologers as cheats.

Astrologers are compelled to predict the future to earn their bread because we expect them to do so.

Astronomy is a science; Astrology, an art; and you, are the subject.

Like a doctor or a lawyer, an astrologer can help only if you share the facts with him.

An astrologer can't predict your future; he can only tell you the position of the stars & their effect, use your logic to balance your future.

We Indians consult astrologers to rid ourselves of negative feelings, just as the Americans & the Europeans visit psychiatrists.

To benefit from an astrologer, be as truthful with him as you would be with a psychiatrist.

Astrology can point you to the cause and you can extrapolate the result accordingly.

To get the best out of an astrologer, tell him all that you have in mind before he tells you what he has in his.

Rituals to counter the ill-effects of stars will benefit ones who believe in them. If you believe in yourself, you don't need rituals.

There is much confusion about astrological predictions. An astrologer's reputation vacillates a lot. Sometimes, he is genuine and at other times a fraudster, depending on his predictions going right or wrong. Not only the person but the profession itself is denounced. When a doctor, engineer or any other professional goes wrong, do we lose our faith in the profession they represent? Likewise, astrology is based on astronomy.

Astronomy is the study of the universe beyond the Earth's atmosphere. Astronomers examine the positions, motions and properties of celestial objects. Astrology attempts to study how those positions, motions and properties affect people and events on Earth.

Therefore, one must correlate the astro-logical (the logic in astrology) predictions with one's own reasoning. Ascertain the astronomical facts and the astrologer's take on the effect these have on you. Don't get influenced by him; you know yourself better than he does.

Don't expect the astrologer to predict the end result, as it depends on you to a large extent. His predictions are based on astronomical facts and the effect they have at large. Your results depend on what you do. In other words,

Life is a sail boat ride.

Wind, the destiny.

But dammit, you are the sailor!

An astrologer can give you the magnitude and the direction of the wind, but it is for you as a sailor to decide how to propel the sailboat to your destination. The astrologer tells you about destiny. You have to benefit from that knowledge to get to your destination.

Before setting off on the Everest expedition, Tenzing and Hillary consulted a priest who told them that neither of them would surmount the Everest and he further predicted that one of them would die during the gruelling expedition. The duo defied the seer's prediction and went on to become the first men to stand atop the world's highest mountain on May 29, 1953.

This is where we need to understand the role of an astrologer. He can predict about our destiny, the course of events that will happen, but he is in no position to assure the result. He can only say what might happen. Ultimately, you are the judge as no one knows you better than yourself. Forewarned is forearmed. We can defy the astrologer. This is what Tenzing and Hillary did. They prepared themselves for the climb to ensure that there would be no surprises for them. Think of a similar instance in your life and you will realise that it was your initiative that propelled you towards your destination.

Climbing the mountain was the less difficult part for Tenzing and Hillary. Making it back to the base camp alive was the bigger challenge. The same is true of life, as stated in the quote below:

Reaching great heights is not half as tough as coming down in life with your sanity intact.

LIFE

Live life as you would savour wine, one sip at a time to get the best out of it.

Make every moment last forever, because nothing else does.

The value of life is best appreciated by those who have only a short time to live.

Enjoy the journey; the destination may not be as exciting.

You would see that life is amusing if you take it seriously.

Dispute is the spice of life.

Don't let your past enslave you. Live for today.

Life would be devoid of excitement if it was all good.

To know God is to know life. To know life is to live it.

Just as the bitter taste of beer can give you a high, so can the bitterness in life turn to bliss.

Just as you enjoy the bitterness of beer, so can you relish life if you cultivate the taste for it.

While leisure and recreation are necessary to get closer to life, you need alertness and effort to face it.

Variety - the spice of life - is the only answer to the law of diminishing returns.

LIVING LIFE LIKE A DOG DOES

Unlike man, a dog lives every moment and dies only once.

Dogs die when they do, whereas we are always dying to do or dying for something before we finally do.

Dogs live till they die, while we die every moment of our lives.

Dogs live every moment because they live by instincts and not by moods.

Both dog and man follow the principal of variety being the spice of life.

Variety is the essence of life. A dog accepts this fact, unlike a man who is bogged down by social norms.

LIFE IS A DILEMMA BETWEEN LIVING A LIE AND SPEAKING ONE

Life is a tightrope walk between speaking a lie and living one.

All human wisdom, be it common sense, spiritual or sublime, tells us to stick to the plain and simple truth. The greatest philosophers and the noblest of men have told us how life is purer and happier when we stay on the narrow path of truthfulness.

Nonetheless, there is a sea of difference between theory and practice. We lead double lives. We present different facets of our personality to different people. We are not averse to bending the truth to suit our purpose.

Why do we do so and to what effect? Does it make us lesser human? Does it make us people with flawed personalities or temperamentally weak?

The dichotomy exists because life itself presents us with a multitude of situations. These situations make it convenient for us to conceal. Man seeks societal approval and many a times, not revealing the truth helps gain acceptance. The pursuit of wealth and material comfort is another factor that goads us to be what we aren't. Then, there are times when we are caught up in emotional attachments. Such entanglements demand a great deal of opacity in our conduct.

Perhaps, the most demanding situation is the one that presents itself as a moral dilemma. For instance, does encouraging a child with positive feedback for a poor performance qualify as a lie? Or does it act as motivation to do better? In this case, the lie does more to put the child on the right path as compared to the brutal truth that might scar her for life.

Moral dilemmas apart, such behaviour sets us off on a path that progressively shrinks our universe. We tend to lose our spontaneity in speech and action. We justify our acts by blaming the world at large for it. Not that there is anything to lose. We often gain the things we set out to achieve by doing so, which makes sense to many of us; because, nothing ventured, nothing gained. It is a material world, after all.

Who is to appear in judgement? Each one of us has their own reasons that no one else can understand.

Better to speak a lie than to live one.

YOU HAVE TO BE AN ACTOR TO FACE LIFE, NOT THE CAMERA

You have to be an actor to face life, the camera needs the real you.

You have to be yourself to face the camera but an actor to face life.

Life is like facing the camera. You would enjoy it if you stopped being conscious of it.

Changing your outlook towards life is like changing the angle of your camera. It changes your view completely.

To live life to the fullest, you have to be a versatile actor to play all the roles.

You are the director of your life. You must know where to throw the light.

Let's admit that we need to be multifaceted to live life to the fullest.

MORE QUOTES ON LIFE

Life is a battle of wits between you and the circumstances. Make them; don't let them make you.

Your life story is an episode of a beautiful script as long as you can watch yourself as a beholder.

Each of us has a purpose in life. We need to know this and play our role accordingly. Play your role well. Don't go against the premise of the story. Follow the best scriptwriter in the world. Who will give you as much flexibility as He does? He gives you the freedom to change your role to make the most of life.

Live life as you would play a game of chess.

There are two aspects to life; living it and facing it. In order to live it, you have to face it.

There is purity in flirting with life.

Only if you flirt with life will you know every aspect of it.

Don't take life seriously; learn to flirt with it.

Freedom is not running away from life but accepting it for what it is.

You're just a puppet. Be wise enough to understand this and smart enough to leverage it.

There is no other way to live life, but to face it.

Life is a sine curve. You have to plumb the depths to soar to the peak.

You can live through love if you learn to dare life's surprises.

Life would be a lot fairer if we ask 'what' instead of 'who'.

Contrary to the general belief, there is logic in every aspect of life. Try using it.

Once we start thinking beyond space and time, we will cease to be anxious about life.

There is nothing clearer than the fact that life is a bundle of contradictions.

The more you try to make sense out of life, the more you realise that it doesn't make sense.

Like love, life cannot be defined because it is entirely subjective.

Don't take life seriously. Flirt, so that you don't get hurt.

Involvement lies at the root of all misery. The only way out is to flirt with life.

Not making assumptions is the only way out in life.

Most of us go through life in a state imbalance, but few realise that equilibrium lies in balancing the heart and mind.

If your mind wants one thing and your heart, another, you will land up with nothing at all. But when the two collaborate, you have everything.

If you are not able to balance your heart and mind, you are imbalanced.

Sleep, shit, shave, shag, swim, sauna, steam and shower are the basic needs after roti, kapda aur makaan.

Everything in life is enjoyable as long as you don't feel guilty about it.

What is flirting with life? It is beyond comprehension. You can only experience it by living life to the fullest.

Flirt with life, so as to not get attached to it.

What if the course of life was so extensive that the ball could never go out of bounds?

Flirting with life is nothing but extending your boundaries.

Don't take anything for granted. Uncertainty is the only certainty!

When we look back, we realize that whatever happened was the only way out.

Life is just a game of Snakes and Ladders. Learn to befriend the snakes.

Happiness is to be found neither in seeking people, nor in places. Instead, flirt with life, the only way out.

Peer pressure is a fact of life; even Raja Ram could not escape it.

Our life should be nothing but a balancing act as per the laws of nature.

We judge people because we adhere to societal norms.

Nimble-witted is the one who keeps peer pressure at bay.

We should be truthful to ourselves and judge the good and the bad accordingly.

You are judgmental because there are social norms to be followed.

We should be governed by the laws of nature and not by the norms of society. By following the norms of society, we are, in fact, defying His norms.

You might lie to the world, but be truthful to yourself.

LOVE & RELATIONSHIP

Love is not everything; it's the only thing.

If it's logical, it's not love.

Love is when every part of me longs for every part of you.

*Every victorious warrior draws his strength from the highest source -
his love.*

When you leave the world, you depart with nothing but your love.

The longer you sustain the latency of your love, the deeper it gets.

Only when you are in love do you get closer to the truth.

I love what happens to me when I think of you.

It's not about you; it's about what I think about you.

*Let's make an opening in the wall we have built around us and enter
it together, my love.*

When I think of you, I smile. Don't ask why.

*Life seems empty all through
I am not half a man without you*

TRUE LOVE IS WHEN YOU RELISH THE ORANGE SHE EATS

Shom is sitting on a dining table chair. The doorbell rings. He opens the door and Raima in a jovial mood walks in.

Raima: Hey Shom, guess what?

Shom goes back to his chair and Raima sits on the chair across him with her elbows on the round dining table, leaning forward as if trying to narrow the gap between them.

Shom: Tell me.

Raima: Nothing. You'll laugh.

Shom: Tell me anyway, I won't laugh..ha.. if you tell me not to.

She looks up at him, he looks at her, tries to control himself and then bursts out laughing. Raima makes a face.

Raima: (sounding annoyed) I won't tell you anything hereafter.

Then she smiles.

Shom: Okay, sorry. Please go on.

Raima: It's about Mentos!

Shom: What's so funny about Mentos?

Raima: Not just Mentos; Honitus too. Both are kept in a big bowl on the receptionist's desk.

Shom: Honey, I only like Honitus, the lesser of the two evils, as it has ginger and honey. Please keep away from Mentos.

Raima: I know you like Honitus and I like Mentos.

Shom: That's just mint and sugar, silly.

Raima: I am silly! So let me tell you what happened today. Something very funny. I left office to meet up with my friends. On my way out, I dug into the bowl as usual.

Shom: Someone caught you doing it?

Raima: No one dare even notice what I do. I'm high up in the organisation.

Shom: (trying to look impressed) Sure, so it seems. Go on.

Raima: (making a face) You keep interrupting and ruin all the fun.

Shom: Sorry. I won't. Please go on.

Raima: (smiling) Yeah, so today I just called some friends and left my work early.

Shom: Early? How could you do that?

Raima: Why not? I don't have any fixed timings. I work late, when I have to. My boss likes my work, calls me a go-getter. She said that with her nose in the air.

Shom: You just know how to handle your boss.

Raima gets offended, makes a face, gets up and walks off. Shom quickly gets up, goes after her, and gives her a loving peck on the cheek.

Shom: Please tell me. I am dying to know what happened.

They both squat on the couch.

Raima: Well, I went out with my friends and we stuffed ourselves with bhajiyas, dahi batata puri and pani puri.

All junk, he thinks and is about to open his mouth but quickly puts a finger on his lips.

Raima: I was feeling a bit burpy, so I fished out the Mentos. All my friends wanted them. I started distributing the Mentos when one of my friends spotted a Honitus. As she went for it, I don't know what happened to me but I actually snatched it back from her. I was shocked at my behaviour, everyone was amazed.

Raima fishes out all the Honitus and puts them on the table. There are only two Mentos among many Honitus. Shom was speechless. He was touched by the purity of her love for him. He hugs her on the couch. She hugs him back. Then, they lie down, she on top of him with her head on his chest. She lifts her head just for a second and says with a smile.

Raima: I'm crazy about you. *Mujhe aise aapke saath kitna sukoon milta hai!* (I am so much at peace with you)

Shom: *Tere sukoon mein hi to mera sukoon hai, pagli.* (And in your peace is mine I find mine, my love).

Just then Raima's cell phone rings. She looks at it and gets a start.

Raima: Oh shit!

Hello, hello, *Pitamaho! Aami bhalo...na, na. Aami aashte parbo na...na. Aami aikhon biye korbo na. Na, aamar kaaj ta aikhane. Pore kautha boli bidaya. (Grandpa! I am good... no..no... I can't come. No, I won't marry now. I have a lot of work here. Talk to you later. Bye.)*

She disconnects but looks defeated and annoyed. Shom looks at her with concern.

Raima: (disgusted) They want me to get married and are using poor grandpa to exert pressure on me. Where were they when I was alone looking after my bedridden mom all these years?

Shom: How long will you be able to resist this? You've been under pressure to marry for a long time.

Raima: You are right. I don't have a choice now.

Shom: Yes, you've just been having sleepless nights and your grandpa is miserable at this age.

Raima: You are right, it is pointless, but what about us?

Shom: Our relationship is like that of Radha and Krishna.

Raima: Oh God! Really?

They both get into a pensive mood, sitting and sulking. Raima slowly comes to Shom and hugs him, breaking into a song.

Raima: (singing)

> *You are my love and I am the precious one*
> *Hug and kiss me more than you have ever done*

> *Wear me like a necklace, an everlasting hug*
> *When you sip your coffee, I want to be the mug*

Every breath of mine is entwined with yours
Your loving touch that my every pore adores

I'll never leave you come what may
I shall come along wherever you say

Live in my heartbeats as you always will
Drive away my sorrow with tact and skill

Shom has tears in his eyes. The atmosphere is heavy with emotion.

THE BALLAD OF SHOM AND RAIMA

Shom and Raima are all by themselves in their apartment in SoBo. There is tension in the air on account of a rift between the two.

Shom: What's wrong with you Raima? How could you keep me waiting for so long? I wonder about your intentions.

Raima: I don't know why you get so worked up. Why don't you read my latest poem instead?

Shom: Crap! How you evade my questions, my concerns! I don't know how I tolerate you. I must have got too accustomed to your ways.

Raima: Then why don't you be nice to me, spoil me a bit? That's the very least you can do for me. I like the way you look at me. Angry man! Come, eat me up.

Shom: You got me there. You want to be one up on me? Or tell the world how smart you are?

Raima: Both!

Shom: You impressed me the day we met. I want you to be

independent. Fight the world, not me. How often must I tell you this?

Raima: Keep trying!

Shom: Don't be my weakness. I want you to be my strength.

Raima: I am your strength. You just wait and watch, you will be proud of me soon.

Shom: I have been waiting for that day.

Raima: It won't be too long now. Have some patience, man.

Shom: Okay we'll see. Do you know how much I worry about you? How much you have led me on? Do you even care for me?

Raima: What do you think? Can't you see? Do I have to keep telling you that you are the only one I have and the only one I care for?

Shom stares at her and she looks back with her enchanting eyes. Her eyes look thoughtful. Her lips part in a smile as she breaks into a poem.

Raima:

> *Get to the depths of my eyes and see*
>
> *You will then know what you see in me*
>
> *But if you don't see what is there in me*
>
> *You don't know love; better learn from me*

Shom:

The look! Oh, I adore the way you look

Killer eyes! The way my heart you took

I dare not look into your eyes, I'll stagger

Your gaze will pierce me like a dagger

Raima:

Why take your eyes away from mine?

My love will suffer, my heart will pine

Don't be afraid, don't abandon me my love

Be together, you as a hand and I thy glove

Shom:

I am not the kind to run away from my position

Our destiny has changed the entire situation

You have changed and are no more the same

I try to come closer but you are never game

Raima:

Though the means have changed

My goal is set, my path arranged

We will be there for a lifetime together

I will not let you go and be yours forever

Shom:

Your path is the same, I am blessed

If your goal is set, I like that the best

Tell me so, let's have faith in each other

If we're in love, let's think together

Raima:

If you could only look into my eyes

And read my mind likewise

The depths will tell you about my compassion

You will then stop asking stupid questions

Shom looks up with a start and smiles. Raima smiles back. They look at each other lovingly. He gets up and hugs Raima tightly. She is equally moved and there are tears of joy caressing her flushed cheeks.

True love is when all differences vanish with mere eye contact.

YOU DON'T CHOOSE TO LOVE. IT CHOOSES YOU.

Love comes without warning and binds you even when you are fully alert.

One thing even a poker face cannot hide is love.

Don't look for love. It is either there or not there.

You don't have to look for love. It's just a glance away.

Don't try to define love, it is beyond definition.

Love is not something you do. You are in it before you know it.

Love in need is love indeed.

Is love without purpose? When I look at you, I lose my sense of purpose.

If you are possessive, you are not in love.

A glimpse of you overshadows my sense of being. Is this love?

I know you. I don't need to know about you.

Love at first sight is a look with the depth that remains with you till the last breath.

The easiest way to love is in finding beauty in everyone and everything you come across.

If you love with your heart, it won't last.
If you love with your head, it's not love.
If you love with both, it's forever.

When the consequences don't matter, you are in love.

True love is causeless; it needs no reciprocation.

Love is blind because it doesn't see reason.

Love is blind. Reason is deaf.
You need both, love and reason to survive.

A true sailor is one who finds love in every port.

Love is the highest form of energy.
It cannot be created or destroyed.
It can only be transmuted.

Love is not for the eyes to see or the ears to hear
It is in the air for you to sense and hold dear

Love is a powerful emotion. It cannot be lost, only transmuted.

Love is infinite. It has no cosmic boundaries.

To love to the fullest is to transcend cosmic boundaries.

Time changes everything but love, because it is timeless.

It's love if it grows with time
Tender, passionate, sublime

A RELATIONSHIP IS OFTEN MISTAKEN FOR LOVE

A relationship with zero obligations is a win-win.

Every relationship is an experiment in the test of life.

One can work on a relationship but never on love.

Love is like a rolling snowball, while a relationship is like an irrevocable fall.

Compatibility - the only issue between man and woman - should be dealt with logically and not emotionally for the welfare of mankind.

Only in the presence of someone special do you let your guard down.

You may love many but be in love with only one.

Our amplitudes may vary. What matters is that our wavelengths match.

When you're in love, you have more than just yourself to live for.

Love tastes sweetest after a rift.

Being true in love is more important than being perfect.

You understand love only when you are exposed to each other's dark side.

It's not about being trustworthy; it's about being trusting.

Trust is the cornerstone of love.

Unless you are trusting, you will not see the purity within.

Only when you trust a soul, will it consider you trustworthy. When both open up, they are open to purity. Anyone you expose your purity to, becomes your soulmate. Love can never be one sided, relationships can.

Soulmate is just a concept. You may have one, some or none at all, depending on how trusting you are.

Being trustworthy may get you love, but to find a soulmate you must be trusting.

Often purity is to be found in the most unacceptable relationships. The word 'acceptable' is purely biased. Just as truth is not acceptable, the alternative truth is.

Base all your relationships on friendship, for it is the most enduring bond.

A pure heart will go to the extent of ending a relationship to keep the love intact.

Even if true love is forever, a relationship may not be so.

A relationship may change with the situation, but true love does not.

Attachment is the ugly face of all relationships. Soulmate is the only relationship devoid of attachment.

True love does not end; what ends is the relationship.

Love has nothing do with relationships because love itself is God.

Maturity in love addresses your insecurity.

The test of true love is changing or doing away with relationships for the sake of love.

Relationships are created, love happens.

While relationships come with responsibilities, love comes with none.

Love is not necessarily about being with the person you share your life with.

TRUE LOVE IS NOT BOUND BY A RELATIONSHIP, NOR IS IT DEFINED BY ONE

Raima had been thinking about Shom all day. How was she going to live without him? Rather, how were they both going to live without each other? Right from the beginning, they had been clear that their relationship could not continue at the cost of hurting their individual families.

She didn't like living in Calcutta anymore. The city had lost its charm, though the club culture prevailed. Grandpa was a member of the *Calcutta Club* and Grandma, 15 years his junior, was a member of the *Saturday Club*.

Shom had an office in Calcutta and usually, he would be in Calcutta at this time of the year. Raima knew he was coming; this time there was more than one reason for him to do so. Being away from each other for close to a month with only FaceTime to keep them connected, they had planned several clandestine rendezvous during his forthcoming visit.

During this time Raima had been introduced to five eligible men and she had rejected them all. She had made it clear that marriage being a commitment for a lifetime, she would be extremely careful in choosing her partner. "A divorce would harm the family's reputation", she would argue to put off her family members.

The pressure to get their only granddaughter married had been playing on her grandparents' minds ever since their daughter-in-law had passed away. They would often remember their only son who had died in a motorcycle accident when Raima was a child.

The sentiments weighed so heavily that Raima started developing cold feet. She did not have the courage, nor could she think of a pretext to go out and meet Shom in the city that now seemed strange. The prospect of managing her overly-fussing grandparents looked increasingly difficult as Shom's arrival at Dum Dum airport drew near.

No sooner had Shom's flight landed, he received a call from Raima. There was a new boldness in her tone. She did not want any surreptitious dealings anymore, she desired freedom. She gave Shom a start by inviting him home the next day on the occasion of Raksha Bandhan. On this day, sisters tie a talisman or amulet called rakhi on the wrists of their brothers in gratitude for protection in times of difficulty. Brothers offer a gift in return. This was very typical of her, thought Shom.

The doorbell rang and Grandma looked up, wondering who it could be. Raima rushed to the door, knowing that it would be Shom. She called out, *"Shomda aapni kaimon aachhen, please come in, eshun boshun (How are you Shomda, please come in, come, sit.),"* as she opened the door and welcomed him.

The grandparents looked alarmed on seeing a middle-aged man enter. Shom was surprised too. He had only half understood her game plan. She winked at Shom to help him relax and get over his awkwardness. Shom nodded at her grandparents, managed a smile and looked around. The atmosphere in the house was serene. It was an auspicious day and Shom reasoned to himself, *"What the hell? Why not?"* He remembered Tapan Ghosh's advice: *You have to be an actor to face life, not the camera.*

He quickly adjusted himself and apologised for visiting without prior intimation. Raima told him about the recent meetings with eligible Brahmin bachelors she had been forced into.

"I don't want to marry, Pitamao is pressurising me. I don't want to be here anymore. For twenty years I have been looking after my dying mother," she said, sobbing profusely.

"He did not come to my help; my aunt was the only one who looked after me. Do they even know what happened to me? What my uncle did to me when I was just thirteen?" she added.

Today, she had no option but to let him know. She quickly got the thali and a beautiful rakhi which she tied to Shom's wrist. Thrilled, he gave Raima his blessings along with a wad of Rs 2000 currency notes, as she applied the traditional vermillion powder on his forehead.

It was an emotional scene. Both grandparents joined in. They were happy about Shom being able to make it to their place despite his busy schedule. They hugged him like a long-lost son. Shom told them that his knowledge of Bengali was limited as he had been living in Bombay since childhood. *"Aami Bangla kauthata bujhte paadi, aito kichu bolte paadi na,"* he added in such a perfect accent that Raima was surprised.

Soulmates can alter their relationship to suit the situation. They go with the flow like a meandering river. This was nothing new for the two, they had done this time and again, to face life and to live it. They had always remained faceless. It was the only way out.

LOVE MAKES WORDS REDUNDANT

If you're really in love, you don't need to say it.

Love is expressed more by deeds than words.

Love is best expressed through body language.

Love is best felt through physical intimacy.

Physical intimacy is the path to spiritual ecstasy.

You can strip her mind naked only if she lets you.

When a woman is being nasty, pay heed! It comes straight from the heart.

There is no greater enjoyment than taming a shrew you love.

Don't rock my boat because we are in it together.

If love is divine, why is a love-child a swine?

Spiritual intercourse takes place when the mind is undressed.

Love and lust; the upper half and the lower half. Emotional togetherness and the physical one. Experiencing the two simultaneously is bliss.

There is no adventure greater than love.

Love is not for the insecure.

ARE SHOM & RAIMA REALLY IN LOVE?

You can read her mind only if she lets you. She will let you only if she loves you.

Shom turns the key and opens the door to his apartment, to see Raima sitting on the barstool. He is surprised to see her there at that time of the day, when she would normally be in her office. As he quietly walks in, he finds her looking disturbed. He is concerned, but decides to underplay his worry.

Shom: Hey! When did you come?

Raima reluctantly looks up as Shom draws closer. She manages a smile.

Raima: A while ago.

Shom comes and stands in front of Raima, whose back is to the bar. He gently caresses Raima's cheek. Touched by the gesture, she reaches out to him in a hug.

Shom: Tell me, what's bugging you? Why so depressed?

Raima: (thinking: Let me tell him the facts) I am fed up. I hate what I am doing.

Shom: Hmm, times are bad for everyone. So just take it easy.

Raima: (thinking: Talk about me, not everyone) It is easy to talk; I would like to see what you would do in my place.

Shom gets up and goes behind the bar. Raima turns the barstool to face him.

Shom: What's your place like?

Raima: (thinking: As if you don't know! Don't fuck with me) Are you making fun of me? You know the bad spell I have been through.

Shom: Please calm down, what's your drink?

Raima: (thinking: I won't get high today) I don't feel like one, not in a mood today. (Thinking: Poor Shom, he wants my company) Okay, give me something alkaline.

Shom: What about Bailey's with crushed ice?

Raima: No, make it Kahlua with crushed ice.

Shom smiles and gets busy with the drinks. He comes back with the drink and places it in front of her. Raima watches him as he fixes himself a perfect mixture of vodka, Bailey's and Kahlua. He clicks his glass with Raima's.

Raima: (thinking: Why is he having my favourite drink?)

Shom: Cheers!

Raima: Cheers! (Thinking: Let me look into his eyes, while I take my first sip) Nice. Refreshing. Now tell me, please don't evade my question.

Shom: You just got agitated; I was not making fun of you.

Raima: (thinking: You were being smart by asking what my place was like) You know what I have gone through; tell me what would you do in my place?

Shom: Well, it all depends on how you look at things. What's good? What's bad? I would like to understand that first.

There is a question mark on Raima's face.

Raima: (thinking: He is just trying to be smart; he is so inconsiderate. Does he love me?) (Pointing a finger at Shom) It is easy for you to talk. You have no imagination. I have gone through hell!

Shom: Don't I know? But sympathizing is not going to help your cause.

Raima: (thinking: Please sympathize with me, love me a bit, and spoil me) (in an angry tone) Please don't say anything if you don't have anything nice to say.

Shom: You look so nice when you are angry like this.

Raima: (thinking: Wow, that's good, he likes me. Let me show some more anger.) (Showing her claws) Grr, I am going to scratch your face. How can you be so rude?

Shom: Ha, ha, how am I rude? I said some nice things about you.

Raima: (thinking: That's not funny. He thinks no end of himself.) You are nasty, you are just enjoying at my expense.

Shom: Enjoying, yes, but not at your cost.

Raima: (thinking: If he is enjoying it, why doesn't he include me in the fun?) Then why don't you tell me the truth?

Shom: It is the purity I see in your expressions. Wah, kya pakeezgi hai!

Raima: (thinking: Yes! Main pakeeza hoon) Wah, kya baat hai! Are you saying that I look beautiful only when angry?

Shom: No, when you are pure. You look enchanting when you have those raw desires. Qudrati husn!

Raima looks sensual and blushes, breaking into a million-dollar smile.

Raima: Youuuu!

Shom intervenes before she says anything.

Shom: Stop! Let me capture this purity. Wow, the way you blush, so real, so pure, so, so beautiful. Sharmeeli! Ba haya!

Raima covers her face with her glass and pretends to take a sip.

Raima: No, please, you know exactly how to manipulate me.

Shom: Whatever I do is in your best interest, isn't it?

Raima: (thinking: Please, no more lectures) What's in my interest?

Shom: The way you look now, so positive, that's all you need to conquer the world. I like to be honest, that's my style.

Raima: (thinking: You are right, but no more lectures please) Okay, okay, spare me the speech and please don't preach.

She sees Shom taken aback and feels bad for him. She calms him down in a friendly tone.

Raima: Talk to me as a friend, your philosophy gets too heavy for me.

Shom: Okay honey, let's talk.

Raima: You were telling me about my bad experience. You said it may not be bad.

Shom: Yes, I said all depends on your mind-set. Bad experience teaches you a lot, because you have to deal with it. It disciplines you.

Raima: (thinking: I know, how your mind works) Good experience teaches you nothing, it just makes you happy and lethargic. No challenges and you take life for granted.

Shom: Wah, kya lajawab soch hai! I am impressed lady; you took the words out of my mouth.

Raima: (thinking: And thoughts out of your mind) Aap mujhe praise kar rahe hain? Ya phir apne aap ko?

Shom: What do you mean?

Raima: (thinking: Smart to aap ban rahe hain) Kyun ke point to aapne hi rakha hai, ke bad experience is good and good experience is not.

Shom: Brilliant! Kya baat hai. Meri billi mujhse meow.

Raima: (amused) Thanks, but I don't agree.

Shom: Don't agree to what? That you are brilliant?

Raima: (thinking: Kyun ke main brilliant nahi hoon?) Of course, I am brilliant.

Shom: Achha! To kya tu meri billi nahin?

Raima: (smiling and purring like a cat) Aur kiski hoon? Meeaaow!

As she leans forward to kiss Shom, he gets a start looking at an exposed part of her breast. Turned on, he caresses her slender neck and boobs before going for her lips. The lips part, revealing the teeth and the tongue. Raima kisses passionately.

Raima: Oh God! Oh God!

Shom: Wow! That was like kissing a pussy. So nice!

Raima pulls herself back and quickly straightens herself.

Raima: How can you behave like this? What if Ramu comes in?

Shom: (whispering) You turned me on. Sorry, what, don't you agree with then?

Raima straightens up.

Raima: That bad is good.

Shom: Hmm, you are trying to be overly smart, aren't you?

Raima reverts to her original frame of mind, defying Shom.

Raima: Nope, only realistic, I know my problems, you don't. You only claim to know them.

Shom: Well, if that's what you claim, do we discuss it out?

Raima: (thinking: I don't want to discuss or even think about my problems anymore) I don't think so, you don't care to understand.

Shom: I think, I do, it is just a bend and not the end. Just move on.

Raima: (thinking: He just talks big) (angrily) What do you want me to do?

Shom: Nothing! Change your attitude, otherwise just shelter the negative side of Raima. Bas, muh phulakar baithi reh.

Shom gets up and walks out of the bar. Raima turns around, her eyes following Shom till he disappears into the living room. The music gets louder, but where do you go to my lovely when you're alone in your bed? Shom concentrates on the music. He leaves her to her thoughts and observes her emotions unnoticed. He is out of her view but she is very much in his.

Shom: (thinking: Shit, this makes me a Peeping Tom, but what the hell; I am sucker for purity of expressions.)

Raima's face turns grim. She looks away and shakes herself out of her mood, expecting Shom to be there. She is disappointed not to see him. She searches for him and calls out to him.

Raima: Where did you go Shom? Please come back.

Shom drags his feet to get back to Raima. He stops in front of her before going behind the bar to refill their drinks.

Shom: Sorry, just dozed off. Main raat bhar soya nahi.

Raima: Poor you, I have the same problem. Main bhi kahaan theek se so sakti hoon. Chalo, zara ek doosre ko relax karte hain.

Shom: Sure, show me the way. (humming) Because you are mine, I walk the line. Shall we go to the bedroom?

Raima: (thinking: That's all men can think of) (smiling) No! Stay here.

Raima turns pensive. She breaks into a poem.

Raima:

> *Dwell in me, as I dwell in you*
>
> *In my thoughts, my dreams, my being too*

If you are with me, by my side

I cast all fears and doubts aside

Shom:

Every breath is a moment in time

That celebrates our love divine

Share with me your sorrow and pain

The heights of love, I thus attain

Raima:

I stand by you, believe in me

Say, how do I prove it to thee

May the world see our shining light

Our love, our strength, Heaven's delight

Shom looks at her. She raises her eyebrows in mock acknowledgement. He cannot suppress a smile.

Shom: I know your mind better than you do because I love you. There's no doubt that you will succeed.

Raima nods in agreement as she hugs him tightly.

YOU ARE IN LOVE, ONLY IF YOU LOVE YOURSELF

How can you love anyone without loving yourself first?

Only when you love yourself will you love others.

True love is all about you and not about the one you love.

Love is bliss only if you are a giver, not otherwise.

Faith in oneself precedes faith in others. This is also true of love.

True love can only be felt, not given or taken.

The test of true love is its eternal nature.

When you give yourself to someone, you get a lifetime of joy in return.

A lie that upholds love is not a lie.

Tell me, what will you gain by reading a book?

Read what's written in my heart, take a look.

The sweetest lessons are the ones we learn when we fall in love.

When you are truly in love, you see love in everyone and everything.

Soulmates are the two sides of a coin, hence completely opposite.

It's never about the person you love. It's about the purity of love that you see within.

It's not about you, it's just about my love for you.

Love is never for your beloved. It is for God through your beloved.

The purity of love that I found in you, I now find everywhere.

Being in love is to experience the purity of the Divine.

The world is full of soulmates if you have the purity to see them.

Purity is reciprocal. Only when both sides open up to one another does purity follow. The bond of soulmates is based on this premise.

We all fall in love with someone. But love sublimates itself when we see the Divine through the one we love.

MARRIAGE, ATTACHMENT AND DETACHMENT

If love has no boundaries, why tie it down?

Marriage is not a union of free souls, but rather, a bondage between two people due to peer pressure.

What destroys a marriage is the marriage itself. It's all about love and not being bound.

Love often culminates in marriage, which often kills it.

Marriage is a bondage created by the insecurities of worldly pressure.

Mutual satisfaction is the bedrock of every marriage.

The easiest way to set the boundaries of two lovers is to get them married.

When in love, you are one as lovers. But when married, you assume two different identities - husband and wife.

Killing your ego is the greatest sacrifice that love demands.

The acid test of true love is the absence of attachment.

Falling in love is binding. It's liberating only if you rise in it.

True love is nothing but detached attachment.

Self-denial is the path to detached love.

Detached love is either causeless or purposeful. Anything in between is mere attachment.
Love if not causeless should only be flirty, as both are detached love.

You are much better off flirting as it is superfluous.

Detached love can only be of two types, purposeless and purposeful.

Love has no concerns; it is only the attachment that does.

It is difficult to balance your mind and body if both are attached to the same person.

Flirting is the perfect appetizer for the meal of love.

Why condemn flirting when it is only an expression of admiration for the opposite sex?

What destroys a marriage is the marriage itself because it is all a commitment, not about love at all.

Detachment is the highest form of love because it is detached attachment.

The only thing fixed about love is its flexibility.

Unfortunately, ego is not self-love but self-attachment.

Love is causeless but with a purpose.

Being in love is a purpose in itself.

Love is a license given by the Almighty while marriage is the one issued by society.

Life is nothing but a game of collecting brownie points. The married will understand this.

HEARTBREAK

The saddest thing about love is that it often goes unnoticed.

Heartbroken? Channelize your sorrow to become worthy of love. The world will be yours.

True love may have a sad ending but not an unhappy one.

True love may have a tragic ending but it remains forever.

Love is often sacrificed at the altar of power.

IS LOVE AN ILLUSION?

Love is not an illusion; death is.

You rise in love if it is your strength otherwise it's only an illusion.

Life is an illusion but love is absolute.

SPIRITUAL LOVE IS POSSIBLE ONLY WHEN YOU UNDRESS YOUR MIND

Raima was in the bedroom, surrounded by her friends and her next-door neighbour. They wanted Raima's advice on the latest fashion trends. Today was the Valentine's eve party but Raima was lost in a world of her own. She couldn't think beyond the heavenly experience she had been through with her valentine only a while ago.

Shom and Raima were in a high spirits that day. They had decided to spend the day in each other's company. Eye contact and expressions were all that they needed to communicate with the other. Nothing was spoken. Given their attuned souls, words were redundant.

Raima touched Shom innocently under his left earlobe but that was enough to send the blood rushing through their bodies. It seemed as if a mere brushing past of the skins was more than the affinity they could sustain. Their bodies shuddered just by holding hands. They felt completely unclad even when veiled. Their souls lay exposed and vulnerable in union. Their eyes met and their excitement levels rose like they could have never imagined. Such heavenly sensations were never fathomed or experienced before.

Perhaps it was a sense of belonging without the possessiveness. Was this spiritual love, a causeless one?

Whatever it may have been, it was pure bliss!

When a simple touch can be so sensuous, a bond so exalting and a restlessness so fierce, an intense sensation takes over. Souls entwine and merge into oblivion, giving rise to serenity and pure bliss.

This happens when we raise our consciousness to our souls. Existence transcends physical, mental and emotional boundaries. All it takes is a casual fondle or a mere glance.

Shom and Raima were in physical contact now, with both hands entwined tightly. The continuity ensured that they were not two bodies but one that was lost to the world and breathing as one. This singular entity would continue in a state of rest unless impressed upon by an external force to change its state. These external forces were none other than the worldly pressures that the subconscious decides to accept, such as a phone call or the ringing of a doorbell.

And so, they did! It was Raima's phone that shook her up and Shom too. She reluctantly answered the call. It was her grandpa.

"Ami dada'r shongair aachi…, na akhoon ashte parbo na…, na dada, amake chede jaabin…, okay, bye," she said. *(I'm with dada…No! I will not be able to come now… No! Dada will leave me home.)*

That evening, Shom and Raima met briefly at the *Great Eastern Hotel* in Calcutta. Shom had come to Calcutta for work, this happened occasionally, perhaps twice or thrice a year. This time around it was willed by Raima who lived there with her grandfather. The two hadn't met in a long time.

As Shom returned to the hotel from work, he found Raima waiting furtively in the lobby.

Shom: Hey sorry, am I late?

Raima (smiling): No, I am a bit early. Let's go up to the room.

That's how it had all started. The phone call seemed to have turned off the magic.

Raima: We don't have much time.

She ran to Shom to unbutton his shirt. He got a start and shook his head gleefully.

Shom: This was too sudden, I don't even have a condom..., my God how to get one now!

Raima: We can't wait.

She pushed Shom on the bed and was all over him in an instant. Grasping intensely and excitedly, it was like two souls colliding against each other. The climax was heavenly and to their surprise, it just continued, cuddled in each other's arms, clutched in a tight embrace, they silently lay alongside each other, in complete bliss.

MOTIVATION

To get the best out of anyone, look only at their positive side.

An iota of positivity is enough to offset a lifetime of negativity.

To be on your feet till the very end is the biggest blessing one can receive.

Unless you forgive yourself, how will you forgive others?

Be positive. The only way out.

Advancement in society is directly proportional to Woman Power.

If controlling your urge to splurge offers comfort to your loved ones, it is the best form of self-denial.

You are at peace only when you have nothing to lose.

Good and bad, the difference is in the way you are influenced to think.

Good or bad,
Who knows that?
Wrong or right,
Who's to decide?

An alter ego is necessary to keep your ego in check.

The best way to ease your anxiety while waiting for a decision is to move into your alter ego.

When you lower your ego, you rise in pride.

When ego and humility join hands, surrender follows. You surge when you merge.

Two partners, taking turns to act as a good and a bad cop, will face any situation effectively.

Women are undoubtedly the stronger sex, yet they want to ape men.

You can always get into a good habit if you don't resist. Make it a habit.

Truth is purposeless.

When you practice, you needn't preach.

A son develops an identity of his own only when he starts understanding his dad.

A child will learn when he sees it happen rather than only hear about it.

Stop nagging your child. Teach him by doing it yourself.

To get the best out of students allow them to pick their own syllabus.

When you feel good about your natural abilities, your personality and your other strengths, negative comments have less power to hurt you.

There is complete justice in nature.
No pain, no gain. You reap as you sow. To every action, there is an equal and opposite reaction.

Do everything to the best of your ability without getting involved, for it leads to attachment.

Why do we get worked up when someone cheats us when we cheat ourselves all the time?

You learn from being ditched. However, there is no learning from ditching yourself.

You have the right connections only if you are connected to yourself.

Better to make a person realise their mistakes than raise their defenses by accusing them.

Praying for yourself is an exercise in vain, someone praying for you is to your gain.

Objects are meant to be used and humans, loved. Sadly, we do it the other way around.

If only the pain bearing capacity of a masochist could be put to productive use, a lot could be achieved.

Each of us is both, an artist and a rationalist. Our individual nature decides the proportion. The wise choose the golden mean.

You step into the light when you are able to share all your dark secrets.

The good part about the bad is that it makes you appreciate the good all the more.

We fail to count our blessings because they come in disguise.

So what if you have an axe to grind, as long as it serves the purpose well.

The habit of passing the blame onto someone is a sign of being dependent on that person.

If everything could be explained, there would be nothing new to learn. A profound thought is like a beautiful woman. It needs no ornamentation.

The more we prosper, the less we flourish.

Purer the soul, wiser the person.

Purity is a measure of innocence.
The outer world teaches us discipline while the inner world is all about purity. We learn to live when we balance the two.

For knowing yourself you have to be unbiased and hence naive.

Wisdom = Foolishness
LHS
Wisdom = Knowing yourself
= Purity = Being Unbiased
= Innocence
= Naivety = Foolishness
Hence
LHS = RHS.
QED.

People who are too trusting are generally not considered worthy of trust.

The trusting type are not considered trustworthy. But if you're not trusting, how will you trust yourself?

Only when you're trusting will you encounter the trustworthy.

If we are not trusting, how will we find anyone trustworthy?

Let's not burden ourselves with labels such as religion, nationality, qualification, profession... Let's stick to the one we are born with: human!
We are born with the label of humanity alone, but we chose to burden ourselves with many.

If we don't discard our roots, we can also flourish like trees and spread our love.

Anyone in a rate race, is similar to rats running helter-skelter. No wonder rats are used as guinea pigs to understand human behaviour.

It's highly immoral to solicit faith by preaching morals.

You are faithful if you respect others for their faith.

Heaven and hell are just concepts, not destinations.

We are always living in our dreams, otherwise what are we living for?

When you are between the devil and the deep sea, have faith and go by instinct.

Ever wondered why we feel compelled to change others and not ourselves?

Advice works best when asked for. Unsolicited advice is no advice at all.

Unsolicited advice amounts to nagging. Set an example for others to follow.

An abstract becomes a masterpiece only when opinionated by influencers.

When you get emotional on realising that you are not the cause of your achievements, you have truly achieved.

A person who is truly receptive generally has faith.

Wisdom dawns on you when you realise that you are a Nobody.

Only when you realise that you are a Nobody, will you become an Everybody.

You distance yourself from the Nobody within as he is the complete opposite of what you should be.

Where to draw a line (Laxman Rekha) is a matter of judgement. This line may be absolute, but it varies from person to person.

We run away from situations because we are forever running away from ourselves.

The only way to control someone is to allow him to control you. Make him dependent on you.

The world expects you to lower your ego without losing yourself in the process.

Don't worry about losing control because you are actually gaining control over your ego.

Mankind seeks solutions in humanity when all other options fail and egos are thoroughly battered. Sadly, this should be the first option.

Intoxication decontrols the mind and sets it free. The challenge lies in harnessing the power of the free mind.

Like happiness, money should be in circulation; the more you give, the more you receive.

A challenge should be accepted only for the fun of it.

All faith is a manifestation of faith in oneself.

Everything happens with a purpose. Don't plan and defeat the purpose.

People who enjoy pain have a lot to gain.

Let's live for the day when the bitter truth tastes sweet.

If you don't correct yourself, you don't love yourself.

If you enjoy correcting yourself, you begin to love yourself.

When you begin to love yourself, you will enjoy correcting yourself.

Don't try to be worthy if you don't want to feel worthless.

Motivation comes from within, it's not something you learn or pick up from others.

He - who does not consider responsibility a burden, nor gets unduly attached to them - alone fulfils these successfully and reaches his destination.

When you feel like laughing at yourself, it shows that you're not defensive, rather, much wiser now.

Like the roots of a tree, the power of the heart lies unseen. Whereas, the power of the mind comes from everyday logic. While the use of the mind is a must, it cannot be at the cost of the roots, without which you're heartless and a living dead.

You are a true giver if your joy lies in someone else's joy.

The real truth, is His opinion known only to those pure of mind.

There's no such thing as a bad or a good period. It is only about being difficult or easy. Good or bad is for you to decide.

If there's a will, there's a way. You only have to pay the price so work for it. Nothing is free.

The purity in an individual will always find purity in others.

Only when you bring down your ego will you see the truth and live with it.

The moods are controlled by ego, insecurity and fear. Let the heart take over.

Purity lies in doing things aimlessly.

Love and passion alone can lead you to purity.

If you cannot stand the traffic light, learn to walk.

How will you live for yourself if you accept to be judged by others?

Faith and patience are overruled by insecurity, which is due to false pride.

When you help someone, you also help yourself. Instead of worrying about how much you get in return, you are better off helping as many people as you can.

When you don't fight boredom, you get into depression, which leads to anxiety in trying to come out of it.

What you say can only be effective if you know who to, how to and when to say it.

It's basic nature and not character, which defines a person.

Be a masochist. Press open the knots from your mind and body. No pain, no gain!

You cannot escape surprises. Keep your reflexes as sharp as those of a cowboy.

Trust yourself to trust others.

Unless you trust yourself, you won't be trusting. How will you then attract the trustworthy?

Own yourself first before you try to own anything else.

The only thing you can own forever is yourself.

Only when you love yourself do you feel the divinity in all creation.

Is building castles in the air not positive thinking?

Basking in the happiness of others is happiness multiplied.

How can you make anyone happy unless you yourself are?

Happy moments are meant to be enjoyed, not shared on social media for likes.

Happiness derived from making others happy is happiness multiplied. Contentment lies in making the environment cheerful.

When you start enjoying the power you have of making others happy just with your smile, you start loving yourself.

Often, we are not happy because we don't want to be.

Why should you look for happiness when it is already within you?

Vivacity from the depth of your soul cannot be described, only experienced.

The pursuit of happiness is the cause of misery. Don't wait for the perfect moment. You will never find one.

When you smile at someone, the person smiles back. According to Newton's third law of motion, 'to every action there is an equal and opposite reaction.'

When we are happy for no reason, why do we question ourselves?

Happiness, like love, is best experienced, not defined.

The greatest cause of misery is the displeasure over the exuberance of others.
Smiles and laughter are contagious; feel free to spread them.

Let's defy space and time to make enjoyable moments last till eternity.

Lower your guard to let happiness in.

Helplessness can be turned to happiness, merely by surrendering.

Make others laugh by laughing at yourself. This is the best way to de-stress.

Happiness is often curtailed by guilt.

Happiness without reason is bliss.

To not have an identity is bliss.
Bliss is when you unite with your inner self.

Bliss is when you have surrendered your worldly self to your inner self.

You are in a state of euphoria when you reveal all your secrets and have no need for privacy.

We live in self-denial; otherwise, we would all be in bliss.

Aimlessness is bliss!

Change nothing, just be yourself to experience peace.

You can't change your life. What you can change is your approach.

Times, they are a-changing. The warriors and thinkers are going to show us the way.

The clock is ticking and the time changing with every passing moment. No one has the answers. Just do it right and you've answered it.

Change with the time, the early birds will enjoy the happy hours.

Changing your perception is the simplest remedy for most of your problems.

All good times must come to an end for change is the essence of life.

Just adapt to the change, the early birds will enjoy the happy hours.

Step out of your comfort zone if you want the New Year to be Happy and New.

You are in control only if you control yourself.

Both, heaven and hell are within you. Choose wisely or to hell with you!

Only when you let go of yourself will the real you surface.

If you only read books, how will you read the scripture inside you?

Be yourself and you shall attain what you seek.

Go all out but don't lose yourself in the process.

Only when you find fault with yourself will you learn.

If you accept yourself the way you are, you are getting close to your higher self.

The more light you emit, the more you enlighten yourself.

Revolution is induced but evolution comes from within.

Don't get worked-up about things happening around you; it's not your doing. Stay focused on yourself.

The real you is what you have always believed in.

Know the devil in you. How else will you encounter him?

When I was not with myself, I was with no one. Now that I'm with myself, I am with everyone else too.

Our purest deeds are those done subconsciously. Otherwise, they are biased.

There is just one person in your life and that's you. Make that person an enemy or a friend, the choice is yours.

Every one of us has only one opponent. Himself!

Let's reduce the differences between me and myself for peace and harmony.

The more you forgive others, the more you respect yourself.

Only if you forgive yourself will you be able to forgive others.

Self-discovery is the gateway to knowledge.

WORK

If you like it, it is not work.

A little distraction often helps you come back with a sharper focus.

You grow only when you groom someone to take your position.

The acid test of real intent is - a glow on your face and a rush of blood in your body.

Belief comes from doing, not reading.

Troubleshooting is the ultimate excitement. If there is no trouble, what will you shoot?

If you are told to do only one thing at a time, how do you function in today's world where you need to multi-task?

SUCCESS AND FAILURE

Only if you are happy with the success of others, will you learn from it.

When the wait is long, it is usually worth waiting for.

You fail because you are taken by surprise. Don't react; reflect instead.

Once bitten, twice alert! Don't shy away.

You win only if you lose your heart.

Better an unsung hero than a fallen star.

A goal has limits but a passion has none.

Worry about today; tomorrow will take care of itself.

You win! I win! It is but no win. If you win or I win, it's no win. The only win is a win-win.

Don't worry about failure, it's the best experience one can gather.

That which can destroy you can also make you stronger if you handle it right.

Fear is conquered by touching rock bottom and not by scaling the heights of success.

GUILT

Guilt is the result of ego. Get rid of it.

There would be no guilt if we could learn to lower our ego.

Regrets are self-created and cause for further regrets.

If you feel sorry for yourself, you are likely to remain that way.

Intuition comes from purity. Purity comes from a guilt free mind. A guilt free mind is a result of self-acceptance.

Unless you make peace with yourself, how will you forgive yourself?

Guilt is the fear of hurting your ego or that of your loved ones.

If you live in guilt, your ego will never allow you to recover.

God has not forbidden any fruit; we have done it to assuage our guilt.

In life the only thing to be concerned about is your guilty conscience.

You are at peace only when you forgive yourself.

Don't feel guilty, do what gives you joy. What makes you think God doesn't want you to enjoy?

By dealing with your guilt, you come close to yourself.

Stop being guilty! In retrospect you will find out that what you did was the best under the given circumstances.

MIND

Unless you build castles in the air, how can you make them?

As you fantasize, so you create.

Pressure and challenge are the best workouts for the mind.

The mind should be as rigid as iron and as flexible as an elastic.

Most of us are potential Steve Jobs! But do we respect ourselves enough to surface?

For every Steve Jobs who acquires fame, there are a million others held back by their own conformity.

You can control your mind if you don't allow others to control you.

Ideas strike you when you are not looking for them.

An empty mind is not the devil's workshop if you control it.

Greater the turbulence, greater is the activity in the mind and body.

Fear kills creativity!

Thought becomes eternal upon finding expression.

The mind can be creative only when it's free of all purpose.

You will have faith only when you see things with an open mind.

A pre-assumed mind leaves free thinking behind.

DESIRE

Craving for what you don't have kills your enjoyment for what you have.

We often exist in no man's land; between the extremities of what we want to be and what we have actually become.

If you don't want more, you have everything.

It is a blessing in disguise when you are looking for something and find something that you should have been looking for.

Isn't it ironic that we want what we don't have and desire what we can't have?

Happiness from the fulfillment of induced desires can only be temporary.

The best way to get something is to not want it at all.

The immediate fulfilment of desires will make you greedy.

FRIENDSHIP

Enemies teach. Friends preach.

There is no truer friend than your own conscience.

The best friendships are cultivated in childhood when we have no ulterior motives.

If you seek happiness in friendship, be an all-weather friend.

HEALTH & WELLNESS

IS TAPAN GHOSH OUT OF HIS MIND?

"When character is lost, nothing is lost;

When wealth is lost, something is lost;

But when health is lost, everything is lost."

Is Tapan Ghosh out of his mind?" asked Khush as he pushed his iPhone towards Harry. *"Look at this quote,"* he said, referring to yet another controversial quote from the maverick.

Harry read it and smiled.

"Why are you smiling? Isn't he mad?" questioned Khush.

"Sure, he is mad! He probably likes it that way," responded Harry.

"Why do you say so?" queried Khush.

"I have read most of his quotes; they're all controversial. But he justifies his madness quite well," said Harry.

"Really? How?" asked Khush.

"He says that good character and bad character is a subjective matter. Come to think of it', reasoned Harry, "How do you judge character?

He asks whether you prefer being judged by your morals or by ethics."

"I see what you mean. One can understand good nature and bad nature. But behaviour, personality and characteristics are too abstract. You have no right to judge, simply because you are not in a position to," replied Khush. *"So why give it so much importance?"* concluded Harry. *"On the other hand, health is well-defined and measurable. To maintain good health, you need discipline, which comes from having a strong mind,"* he added.

"That's Tapan Ghosh's view as well. He says that looking after your health should be your prime goal," said Khush.

"Absolutely! In fact, he has said several things about health, all of which are pertinent. Some of these may sound controversial, but the truth cannot be denied," commented Harry.

"Do you remember his take on religion?" asked Khush.

"Of course! He says that health is the only religion that matters. Every other religion is fake. Now, this may sound blasphemous, but it cannot be denied. You can't practice any religion if you are not in sound health," said Harry.

"He goes on to say that a true man of God is one who keeps himself physically, mentally, emotionally and spiritually healthy. Now, can anyone deny this?" continued Harry.

"Not at all. But tell me, how does one define health?" enquired Khush.

"Tapan Ghosh has an answer to this question too. Health is the sum total of physical well-being, mental stability, emotional soundness and finally, spiritual enlightenment. Can you beat that?" asked Harry.

"Wow! Tapan da has studied health in great detail. He has summed it up beautifully," remarked Khush. *"Does he say anything about its benefit?"*

"He says that sound emotional health can handle any crisis," said Harry. *"True But how does one keep fit?"* enquired Khush.

"According to Tapan da, to keep physically fit, listen to your body, not to somebody. We do the complete opposite. For example, the human body is designed in accordance with the laws of nature. The British left behind their potty which goes against these laws. It induces constipation, causes faecal stagnation, enlarges the prostate, leads to infection and weakens the muscles of the lower body," said Harry. *"Anything else that he suggests?"* asked Khush.

"He has a lot to say in this regard. All sound advice. As you open your eyes in the morning, the first thing to do is what the dog does. Stretch! Twists and turns are necessary to keep your body and mind fit. So is it with your face; you are at liberty to make faces," recalled Harry.

"You mean, smile all the time, be cheerful," added Khush.

"Right! If you now link Tapan Ghosh's take on character - When character is lost, nothing is lost; when wealth is lost, something is lost; but when health is lost, everything is lost — to his thoughts on health, you will realise that he is talking sense. None of what he says is controversial or thoughtless. On the contrary, many who criticise him are out of their mind," concluded Harry with a smile.

SPIRITUALITY

Only when you connect with yourself, do you interact with the beyond.

There is only one true way to connect with God. Your own way.

True self-denial is always for the sake of love. If the love is for yourself, you are one with God.

Thank God that He doesn't listen to you every time. He knows what's best for you.

You scratch my back and I scratch yours is the universally accepted fact and also your relationship with the Almighty. The difference is He knows where to scratch and you don't.

Whenever you await God's decision, don't be anxious. Go into another plane or another identity.

A win-win situation is God's will.

We all are God's messengers; no one is the chosen one.

Sex is God's gift to mankind. If we don't understand this, how will we understand God?

What is history but the power struggle between rulers and Godmen!

Ego comes from worldly influence. Spirituality knows this and rises above.

We don't see God in others because it is easier to see the Devil in them.

Is God an outsider?

If not, what's the worry?
If yes, why worry?
The issue is not about God being with you, as He is with everyone without discrimination. The question is 'Are you with God?'

God is not a variable entity but a constant phenomenon.

He speaks to you only if you would listen.

A true man of God is the one who keeps himself physically, mentally, emotionally and spiritually healthy.

Any give and take with God must be direct; never through a middleman.

Blessings from anyone are, in fact, blessings from God.

We spend all our lives in search of a mirage. We want to be what we are not without realizing the value of what we are. We go looking for God, not realizing that Godliness is within us.

By running away from ourselves, we are running away from truth, purity and God.

God doesn't care if you're not trustworthy, He wants you to be just trusting.

If God is in each one of us, why don't we accept the divinity in the people around us?

If God had his will, we would all have a win-win situation.

Let's follow our own religion because God is in each one of us.

If we say that God is all-encompassing, we must have the faith that He is in each one of us.

The day you trust yourself, you will trust God.

God is willing to meet you half way. Just walk the other half.

God is in total agreement with you. Are you in total agreement with him? What would you agree to, unless you know what he wants?

Build your reserves by all means but they are safest with God.

God wants us to make things happen but not at the cost of ruining ourselves.

Why not just go with His plan?

Yes! We all have one God, the one inside each one of us. Is your God the same as mine?

A win-win is nothing but balancing act of God.

We don't believe in destiny because we don't trust God.

Being attached to oneself is ego. Loving oneself is loving God.

Neither man nor machine, can replace its creator.

The moment you fear God, He is not God!

Most of the sins are committed in the name of God. Buying and selling of favours in the name of God is a remunerative business.

Both the eyes are one-sided. For the perfect balance, you need Shiva's third eye.

Beyond our vision is the fourth dimension which can only be seen with Shiva's third eye. You have to balance the left and the right eye to get there. This can only be done with a totally empty mind.

There's a lot to steal from the scriptures of the Almighty without being accused of plagiarism.

Repeated reading of religious scriptures is not prayer; absorbing them is.

Absorbing the scriptures inside you is more virtuous than reading a prayer book.

How do we expect to reach God by bribing Him or beating drums in the middle of the night?

How can anyone be free of corruption in this country, when extortion is done in the name of God?

God created man. Man corrupted God.

There is nothing in God's hands! Everything has been given to us. No wonder we have made a mess of it.

By following the norms of society, we are in fact defying His norms.

God wanted only one relationship between Him and us, but we have complicated that too.

All the battles have been fought only to impose your perception of God on others, though God is too private to be shared.

The Devil in us has created God to justify our actions.

The only conflict that's healthy is the one between God and you.

You are lucky if you are used by someone because God is using you to serve him.

OTHER QUOTES

Some people want to be in vogue even at the cost of being a rogue.

Comparison is the root cause of insecurity.

Everything is fair in love and war but war is not fair.

A fool is not cut out for this world and a shrewd man has no place in the world beyond.

Rather be called a fool and a coward than to prove otherwise.

A fool does not know that he's a fool simply because he's not one. You are.

Although in bliss, being devoid of peer pressure, simpletons are considered misfits.

You decide for yourself is not as casual as it sounds.

Take only as much as you need. Anything more is nothing but greed.

Do you prefer being judged by your morals or by ethics?

Good character and bad character is a subjective matter.

Perceptions can be highly damaging. What good is it if you are loved or hated for what you are not?

Old is not gold; don't live in the past.

Is a philanthropist a person trying to get rid of unwanted money to build a reputation or the guy of modest means trying to put a smile on the face of a deserving man?

That which is forbidden, is desirable.

Banning something is the easiest way to make it desirable.

Social and legal acceptance of anything that is taboo brings down the demand for it.

If you draw the gun and don't shoot right, you are shot down!

You can have your cake and eat it too if you are able to eat half and save half.

Is a camera as precise as the human eye? No way, it is not empowered by the brain.

Fiction is nothing but non-fiction couched to conceal the identity of the writer.

Non-fiction is, in fact, fiction most of the time unless you live it before you write it.

Impatience is a virtue if you have to write for today's generation.

Writing a story is quite easy, because the writer is doing all the talking in one language. There're no dialogues as such. Moreover, he writes, what the characters think.

A novice writer reads a lot to learn to write. He would be better off thinking of what to write.

A writer has to live it up to capture the reader's imagination.

Drama with a sprinkling of reality is pure entertainment. Docu-drama, which is the reverse of this, is equally entertaining.

Many of us suffer from the dark complexion of a white-skin complex.

The tongue is like a fiery flame.

In the quest for perfection, we often forget that the very purpose of language is to communicate.

Body language, tone and expressions are purer than written language which is subject to rules and intricate vocabulary.

You cannot master a language unless you experience the culture.

When you go to a place where you don't understand the language, you may be better off understanding people by their actions. The heart speaks louder than the mind.

'Care a hang' attitude maybe the best to adopt when faced by empty threats.

We expect people to change without realizing that they are better off not listening to you.

Man's biggest fear, the fear of death, can be overcome by his thirst for knowledge of death.

Faith in fate is possible only if you are the trusting kind and not concerned about being labeled untrustworthy as a result.

Distrust in others points to the lack of self-belief.

If you are the trusting kind, you are not considered trustworthy.

Those who are trusting are considered gullible, although trustworthy.

Those who have faith in their fate are trusting but considered gullible.

You can have a good understanding with dogs and horses. Not with monkeys. For that, you have to be trusting as they are not considered trustworthy.

If you stay on your toes, chances are you will die on your feet.

Sadly, not being seen as a wrong doer is more important than the real you.

There are two kinds of people. One takes pleasure in bearing physical and emotional pain while the other draws pleasure from inflicting it.

The most distinct definition of good and bad is the one between a masochist and a sadist.

Whether we like it or not, each one of us leans towards sadism or masochism. However, the extent varies from one individual to another.

Faith is often mistaken for gullibility.

If an artist truly expresses himself, he is likely to get rejected.

An atheist is also a believer. The difference lies in the object of belief.

We Indians accept all religions only so that we may enjoy every festive holiday.

*Unsolicited advice is always considered worthless.
Unsolicited help amounts to interference.*

We must involve people when they are needed, else they will involve themselves when they are not needed.

Man, as a bread earner, is insecure because the measure of his success lies with his better half.

Men want variety and women want possession. This is the fundamental difference between the two.

Balance is the word that best describes the universe.

When the laws of nature are all about harmony, we adamantly live in a state of disharmony, as we like to differentiate between caste, creed, religion, traffic rules and even the units of measure.

Newton's First Law of Motion clearly differentiates between morals (God's will) and ethics (peer pressure). Everybody continues in a state of rest or uniform motion (morals) unless compelled to change that state by forces impressed upon it (ethics).

For every action there's an equal and opposite reaction. Reclaim the sea, it will claim back the land.

All the disharmony in the world is due to interference with the harmony in nature.

The choice is clear. Adhere to social norms and burn out or be an outcast. Therefore, the only way forward is to practise double standards.

The more you illuminate, the better you capture.

Should the measure of a man be the number of mourners at his funeral? What if he was not close to anyone but himself?

You are in a sorry state if you feel sorry for yourself.

We can only sympathize with people who feel sorry for themselves. Respect is reserved for those who respect themselves.

Animals are free because they can't pick and choose.

If the ambience is right, you'll get your high on a mocktail in a cocktail glass, as it is a guilt-free drink.

Not fighting for our rights is a crime in itself.

Sometimes, humility is ego in disguise.

A person free of ego is often mistaken for a simpleton.

Being thick-skinned often lightens the burden of ego.

The hallmark of a thick-skinned person and a fool is the lowering of their ego.

The acid test of conquering ego is to love what you hate.

There are two of you in you, let both coexist.

Every one of us has an alter ego that keeps monkeying around.
You can survive but not live with a single identity.

Why is 'I' always in capital?
It represents superego.
Your identity is your superego that leads to the 'I' in you. If you go
with your alter ego the 'I' changes to 'we' - a balanced ego.

Shiva and Bajrangbali, morals and ethics, liberal and conservative,
id and superego. Society tends to be rightist; we need to balance the
two.

Every individual has the traits of both, Shiva, a Nobody, and Bajrang,
a Somebody. Only the proportions vary.

Ego gets distributed when you have more than one identity just as
your attachment gets distributed when you have more than one child.

1 identity = I, I = ego
2 identities = we, we = ego/2
3 identities = we, we = ego/3
And so on...

The mind asserts, therefore it's a 'Somebody'. Whereas, the heart loves
silently, therefore it is a 'Nobody'.

Between Nobody and Somebody, one has to be faceless. While Nobody
is naturally faceless, for Somebody to be faceless he has to be a criminal
or a saint.

Most of us think only as Somebody, without considering or knowing about Nobody.

A Nobody will match up to Somebody, if he is able to join hands with another Nobody, a soulmate!

Somebody is just one thing and Nobody, nothing. Together, they are everything.

When Somebody says he got lucky, he's on the path of acknowledging the doer within; the Nobody.

You= Somebody; an identity who's a living dead. You= Nobody; not an identity, dead to the world. You = Somebody + Nobody= Everybody You don't love yourself, you are just attached to yourself, that's ego. Bring down your ego to bring up your pride.

Ego is being attached to oneself, whereas loving oneself is loving the divine within us.

The clearest definition of good and bad is that of a masochist and a sadist.

Why undo nature when this is the cause of all the problems the world over?

It's time we reciprocate the faithfulness of dogs in our neighborhood than hanker after pedigrees.

I may be adding years but the best part is, my thinking has not matured.

It is a sad commentary on our education system that students commit suicide to acquire knowledge that is available at the tap of a key.

When you are not trusting, you won't find anyone or anything trustworthy. This insecurity leads us to complicate everything. Any arrangement or agreement we have with others goes into thousands of pages due to red herrings created by imaginary fears. Despite taking all possible measures, they often go into litigation. This is how everyone from media to law makes money.

If English is here to stay, the least we Indians can do is to promote Hinglish. The best of two languages will make Hinglish user-friendly. Newborns are pure souls, the Nobodies, who gradually develop their individuality and eventually become Somebodies.

Why are we being correct at the cost of being true to ourselves?

Being in circulation holds good for every fluid in your body. This works for everything else too.

Doing nothing - not even digging your own grave - is in fact, digging it.

You will be digging your grave, if you do nothing. Better start digging it!

You are safe well within the boundary but you miss out on a wider periphery.

In the era of gender equality, we see women smoking and men sporting pony tails.

Everything else in life can be confusing but what is clear is the importance of looking after yourself.

Ego is nothing but self-attachment, which is Somebody, while self-love is Nobody.

Fight with nature and you are gone. Go with it and you are on.

Coming in the way of others is a sin we commit all the time.

How can a trustworthy person believe anyone who is not trusting?

Soliciting faith is an immoral act emanating from insecurity.

OF MONKEYS AND MEN

Have you heard of a man being stopped in his tracks by a giant monkey? What I am about to narrate is no story or figment of imagination. It actually happened to me.

It was in the middle of nowhere that I encountered a strange and seemingly dangerous situation that made me question our pre-conditioned thinking. Why do we respond to situations in a certain set fashion? Is it because we have been told to unquestioningly judge right and wrong based on certain ambiguous parameters? Do our instincts turn to insecurities? Do they create distances between us and others, rather than cocoon us from the unknown? Here's an incident that triggered these questions.

25 km from Rishikesh, the Vashistha Cave is named after Rishi Vashistha, guru of Lord Rama and manas putra (human progeny) of Lord Brahma. One of the saptarishis (seven great sages) of ancient times, it is believed that Vashistha meditated and lived here till the age of 85 when he attained nirvana.

Having visited the cave, I was walking down the path that connected it with the approach road. The vibrations I had felt there – coupled with the serene environment – had a calming effect on me. Lost in thought, I didn't realise that a giant monkey had parked itself further ahead, blocking my path, until we were a couple of feet apart. A sense of panic gripped me. I froze, fearing that any movement on my part might antagonize it. An eerie silence enveloped us.

Getting into an impasse

"We keep away from monkeys because they represent the real us who

we refuse to acknowledge."

For what seemed a long time, there was no movement on either side. It was a tense situation. I had to get away but running wasn't an option. Worse, any movement on my part evoked a similar response from the ape. We had reached an impasse.

Several agonizing moments later, I started all over again, I took two tentative steps, only to see the monkey match my action. But the impasse had been broken. The mind and body were in sync again. I took another step and the monkey did the same.

As I kept going, I could see the monkey keep pace with me. Our movements seemed to be synchronized. The mind was racing with several thoughts. What must I do next? How should I shake him off my trail? I started walking towards the main road; he alongside, a bit concerned as this was not his regular beat. I felt slightly relieved that I had managed to make it thus far without aggravating the primate.

An unexpected call

"Only those who love themselves will love monkeys as pets."

But my problems weren't over yet. Suddenly the phone in my pocket began to ring. I quickly turned it off as I saw him getting worked up, teeth bared, screeching shrilly, all poised to attack. It was scary. The renewed silence calmed him down and we continued our synchronized walk.

The mind was planning an escape out of this strained situation. We were now in safer territory, but there were no people close by. A few in the distance were too far to call out to, without running the risk of agitating my walking partner. I shook my head at my helplessness. He shook his head too, seemingly in mock concern.

Relief at hand

"Aren't we monkeys at heart? Don't we like to monkey around? Each one of us has an alter ego that keeps monkeying around."

Suddenly, my car arrived. I figured that it must have been the driver who had called a few moments earlier. My friend got a startled. I quietly went ahead, opened the rear door and with a wave of my hand, signalled him to join me in the car. I almost broke out into laughter as he did the same. Confrontation had given way to courtesy. Pushing my luck, I extended the invitation one more time. After you, he gestured. Seizing the opportunity, I jumped into the car and slammed the door shut before he could follow me. The driver shot off immediately.

From the safety of the moving vehicle, I turned back to see a puzzled look on the monkey's face. Strangely, I wanted to go back. Picking up a stem of bananas from a vendor down the road, we returned to the spot where we had left him. He was still there.

Clearing the misunderstanding

"We often talk about mind over matter, not realising that sometimes it is the monkey in us over mind."

I stepped out of the car and walked towards him. Puzzled at my hasty exit, the monkey followed my every move. Our eyes were now locked in contact. I walked as close to him as my instinct would permit. Placing the bunch of fruit on the edge of the road, I waved my arm, inviting him to partake of the feast. He didn't budge an inch. His eyes were still locked on mine.

I was no longer afraid. Turning away, I calmly walked back to the car. As we drove away, I turned around to see the monkey approach the pile of bananas. He pulled one off the stem, unpeeled it and bit into it. He looked pleased as he relished the first bite. Perhaps he now realized that I wasn't a foe after all.

I felt a sense of relief too. Our initial confrontation had turned into an unspoken understanding. Our own insecurities prevent us from understanding others, be it humans or other creatures. I came away feeling that we might be able to understand other people better if we attempt to understand animals first.

This was my first major interaction with a monkey. Thereafter, there have been few more chance meetings.

Once, when two tiny monkeys entered my window after ransacking my neighbour's house, I remained calm and was prepared for them. They just looked at me and quietly went back the way they had come from.

By and large I have noticed people are scared of monkeys as they're quite unstable and difficult to predict. We may identify with dogs, but not with monkeys. This is because we do not want to identify with monkeys. We don't want to face the truth that we have evolved from them.

"We do not tolerate any monkey business because we dare not revel ourselves. We hate monkeys. They are so unstable. Bloody copycats!"

www.ingramcontent.com/pod-product-compliance
Lightning Source LLC
Chambersburg PA
CBHW051220160726
47994CB00002B/674